what is sport?

WHAT IS SPORT?

roland barthes TRANSLATED BY RICHARD HOWARD

yale university press   new haven and london

Copyright © by Les Presses de l'Université de Montréal.
Translation copyright © 2007 by Yale University.
Translator's Afterword copyright © 2007 by Richard Howard.
All rights reserved.

Designed by Sonia L. Shannon. Set in Bulmer by Integrated Publishing Solutions.
Printed in the United States of America.

Library of Congress Cataloging-in-Publication Data
Barthes, Roland.
[Sport et les hommes. English]
What is sport? / Roland Barthes ; translated by Richard Howard.
    p.   cm.
ISBN 978-0-300-11604-5 (pbk. : alk. paper) 1. Sports. I. Title.
GV707.B37713 2007
796.01—dc22   2007021290

A catalogue record for this book is available from the British Library.

The paper in this book meets the guidelines for permanence and durability of the Committee on Production Guidelines for Book Longevity of the Council on Library Resources.

10 9 8 7 6 5 4 3 2 1

CONTENTS

What Is Sport? is the text of a short, intriguing Canadian documentary film called *Le Sport et les hommes.* The film is the product of a collaboration between two great writers, a French author whose reputation in 1960 was already established and a Québécois writer still finding his way. Roland Barthes had already published two texts capital in twentieth-century French cultural history—*Writing Degree Zero* (1953) and *Mythologies* (1957)—in the latter of which he specifically discussed wrestling ("In the Ring") and bicycle racing ("The Tour de France as Epic"). Hubert Aquin was not yet the novelist of *Prochain épisode* (1965) or *Neige noire* (1974) and was known (exclusively in Québec) only as a contributor to the periodical *Liberté.* Yet from the start Roland Barthes generously agreed to collaborate with Aquin on what was only, as yet, a project for a film, first by letter and then in person, in Paris but also in Montréal.

It was in the spring of 1960 that Aquin, then a producer at the National Film Board in Montréal, read *Mythologies.* Had the project of a documentary film about sports already occurred to him or was it the reading of Barthes's essays that gave him the idea? In a letter dated April 4, 1960, in which he proposes that the French critic write a commentary for his film (provisionally titled "Le Sport dans le monde"), Aquin suggests that it is more or less a coincidence, the fortuitous encounter of a reading and a desire. In any case, the encounter occurred and soon bore fruit.

Conditioned in part by the formula imposed by the series *Comparaisons,* in which the documentary would appear, Aquin's intention was to present five national sports as a "social and poetic phenomenon." He was thinking of bullfighting in Spain, car races in Italy, soccer in Hungary, hockey in Canada, and the Tour de France bicycle races. The choice of the countries represented was to change in the course of production, but the lineup of sports was determined at this time. Barthes accepted the invitation—he would write the commentary which follows, and Aquin would be responsible for the visual editing; rather than photograph new sequences, he would construct his film from archival material and from newsreel sequences purchased from many sources.

Their collaboration continued by letter until two working meetings in the early 1960s. The first occurred in autumn 1960 in Paris; from September 27 to November 1, Aquin worked with Barthes on the realization of their project. He then invited Barthes to Québec in order to continue the work, meanwhile arranging a series of university lectures and television interviews for his distinguished guest. Barthes arrived in Montréal on January 16, 1961, for a stay of about two weeks that would familiarize him with a sport that figures in the background of the film's title sequences but which he knew only slightly: ice hockey. The artists' collaboration continued until April through the support of the studios of the National Film Board in London. The film was completed, as *Le Sport et les hommes,* and was shown June 1, 1961, as part of the series *Temps présent* on the television network of Radio Canada. The following year it won the Producer's Prize at the Cortina d'Ampezzo Festival in Italy.

The correspondence between Barthes and Aquin affords information about how the project developed, specifically concerning the French critic's role in its orientation. We learn among other things that he is responsible for the final title. After proposing "something simple and direct like *Vive le sport*," and then a series of "hardly original" titles, two of which he prefers—*Sport, miroir des hommes* and *Sport, miroir de l'homme*—Aquin finally retained the fourth title on the list. The first title Barthes proposed, *Qu'est-ce que le sport?* (What is sport?), became the film's leitmotif, cited in both the prelude and the finale and implicit throughout the commentary.

It is thus a testimony both to sport and to man that we offer readers today, a testimony that must be read for what it claims to be: new mythologies. This text was not published in the Seuil editions of Barthes's *Oeuvres complètes*—neither the three-volume version of 1995 nor the five-volume edition of 2002. This short, haunting book will appeal to all lovers of Barthes's work curious enough to read the mythologist's thoughts, some years after *Mythologies,* about sports as, or beyond, myth; to readers of Hubert Aquin's work who will recognize a creator already dealing with questions that would be the basis of his future texts: nationality and freedom; and to sports enthusiasts interested in a deeper, philosophical understanding of the role of sport in modern society.

The commentary of the film *Le Sport et les hommes* is the result of unanticipated but sustained exchanges that shed new light on the respective works of its two creators. It is, above all, one of the first contributions to a body of thought destined to occupy generations of commentators, concerning sport-as-spectacle ("spectator sports"). That is why it must be published.

GILLES DUPUIS

The correspondence exchanged between the collaborators—fifteen letters and one telegram—may be found today in the Fonds Andrée Yanacopoulo of the ÉDAQ archives in the University of Québec in Montréal. Our gratitude to Jacinthe Martel, in charge of the ARCHÈ project (Centre québécois de recherché sur l'archive littéraire) of the University of Québec in Montréal for permission to consult and reprint this correspondence.

WHAT IS SPORT?

DIRECTOR Hubert Aquin

TEXT Roland Barthes

NARRATOR Robert Gadouas

MONTAGE Robert Russell

MUSIC Al Baculus

MUSICAL MONTAGE Malca Gillson

SOUND Kathleen Shannon

MIXING Ron Alexander

GENERAL DIRECTION Guy Glover

Post-production script
August 2nd 1961

What need have these men to attack? Why are men disturbed by this spectacle? Why are they totally committed to it? Why this useless combat? What is sport?

Bullfighting is hardly a sport, yet it is perhaps the model and the limit of all sports: strict rules of combat, strength of the adversary, man's knowledge and courage; all our modern sports are in this spectacle from another age, heir of ancient religious sacrifices. But this theater is a false theater: real death occurs in it. The bull entering here

3

A man alone, with no other weapon than a slender beribboned hook, will tease the bull: call out to him . . . stab him lightly . . . insouciantly slip away.

ourage, knowledge, beauty,
ese are what man opposes
the strength of the animal,
s is the human ordeal,
which the bull's death
ll be the prize.

will die; and it is because this death is inevitable that the bullfight is a tragedy. This tragedy will be performed in four acts, of which the epilogue is death.

First, passes of the cape: the torero must learn to know the bull—that is, to play with him: to provoke him, to avoid him, to entangle him deftly, in short to ensure his docility in fighting according to the rules.

Then the picadors: here they come, on horseback at the far end of the ring, riding along the barrier. Their function is to exhaust the bull, to block his charges in order to diminish his excess of violence over the torero.

5

Act Three. The banderillas.

A man alone, with no other weapon than a slender beribboned hook, will tease the bull: call out to him . . . stab him lightly . . . insouciantly slip away.

Here comes the final act. The bull is still the stronger, yet will certainly die. . . . The bullfight will tell men why man is best. First of all, because the man's courage is conscious: his courage is the consciousness of fear, freely accepted, freely overcome.

Man's second superiority is his knowledge. The bull does not know man; man knows the bull, anticipates his movements, their limits, and can

7

. . . the crowd tossing him flowers and gifts, which he graciously returns . . .

lead his adversary to the site he has chosen, and if this site is dangerous, he knows it and has chosen it for this reason.

There is something else in the torero's style. What is style? Style makes a difficult action into a graceful gesture, introduces a rhythm into fatality. Style is to be courageous without disorder, to give necessity the appearance of freedom. Courage, knowledge, beauty, these are what man opposes to the strength of the animal, this is the human ordeal, of which the bull's death will be the prize.

Furthermore what the crowd honors in the victor, tossing him flowers and gifts, which he graciously returns, is not man's victory over the animal, for the bull is always defeated; it is man's victory over ignorance, fear, necessity. Man has made his victory a spectacle, so that it might become the victory of all those watching him and recognizing themselves in him.

And what do they recognize in the great car racer? The victor over a much subtler enemy: time. Here all of man's courage and knowledge will be focused on one thing: the machine. By the machine man will conquer, but perhaps by the machine he will die. So that here the relation between man and the machine is infinitely circumspect: what will function very fast must first be tested very slowly, for speed is never anything but the recompense of extreme deliberation; first of all,

11

What will function very fast must first be tested

very slowly . . .

the gears must be verified, for a great deal will be asked of them: up to 2,500 changes of speed an hour; the site of the competition must also be carefully checked, the track first of all, its angles, its curves, its levels . . .

Next, in order to try it out, to race alone, with no other enemy but time, and to confront in this effort both the machine and the terrain together, for it is all three at once that the racer must first of all conquer before triumphing over his human rivals.

Finally and above all it is the engine that must be prepared and where we find an embarrassment

Once the race starts,

an implacable economy

will govern each atom

of movement, for time is

henceforth everywhere.

of riches, much like those found in an inspired brain: here twelve sparkplugs must be changed every five laps.

We are at Sebring in Florida; this is a twelve-hour race among different types of cars. Once the race starts, an implacable economy will govern each atom of movement, for time is henceforth everywhere.

On straight drives, it is the motor's effort that is most important, yet this effort remains human in its way: in it are deposited the labor, the inventiveness, and the care of dozens of men who have prepared, refined, and checked the most difficult of equations: an extreme power, a minimal resistance, whether of weight or of wind.

But on the turns, apart from the machine's suspension, it is the racer who does everything; for here, space is against time. Hence the racer must be able to cheat space, to decide whether he can spare it . . . or if he will brutally cut it down;

On the turns . . . space is against time.

and he must have the courage to drive this wager to the brink of the impossible.

It is not only the racer who struggles against time, it is his whole team. At Sebring the track is a former airfield, on which tires are quickly worn down; some teams manage to change them in a minute and a half: to them too belongs a share of the final victory. In this combat against time, terrible as the consequences may sometimes be, there is no fury: only an immense courage focused on the inertia of things. Hence the death of a racer is infinitely sad: for it is not only a man who dies here, it is a particle of perfection which vanishes

This is the meaning of a great automobile race: that the swiftest force is only a sum of various kinds of patience, of measurements, of subtleties, of infinitely precise and infinitely demanding actions.

By the machine man will conquer,

but perhaps by the machine he will die.

from this world. But it is precisely because such perfection is mortal that it is human. No sooner is everything lost in one place than other men will begin again in another.

Here is the start of one of the world's Grand Prix races: it is a crucial test, because the more powerful the machine, the heavier it is, and from this paradox the greatest speed must be derived: hence there is no starter on these cars: to suppress a few kilos is to gain a few seconds.

It is these preparations for starting that give the car race its meaning: that of a victory over weight and the inertia of things. At rest, these cars

The death of a racer is infinitely sad: for it is not only a man who dies here, it is a particle of perfection which vanishes from this world.

are heavy, passive, difficult to maneuver: as with a bird hampered by its wings, it is their potential power that weighs them down. Yet once lined up, approaching their function, which is combat, they already become lighter, grow impatient. . . . Once started, these machines will gradually transform their mass into agility, their weight into power; no sooner are they in their element, which is speed,

The track is a former airfield, on which tires are quickly worn down; some teams manage to change them in a minute and a half. In this combat against time, there is no fury: only an immense courage focused on the inertia of things.

21

To stop is virtually to die.

than they will wrap the entire world in it, on the most varied tracks and circuits: at Nürburgring, the most dangerous; at Monaco, the most tortuous; from Monza, the most exhausting, to Spa, the fastest.

To stop is virtually to die. If the machine fails, its master must be informed of the fact with a certain discretion. For a great racer does not conquer his machine, he tames it; he is not only the winner, he is also the one who destroys nothing. A wrecked machine generates something like the sadness caused by the death of an irreplaceable being, even as life continues around him.

This is the meaning of a great automobile race: that the swiftest force is only a sum of various kinds of patience, of measurements, of subtleties, of infinitely precise and infinitely demanding actions.

What this man has done is to drive himself and his machine to the limit of what is possible. He has won his victory not over his rivals, but on the contrary *with them,* over the obstinate heaviness of things: the most murderous of sports is also the most generous.

These machines will gradually transform their mass into agility, their weight into power; no sooner are they in their element, which is speed, than they will wrap the entire world in it.

Each year, in July, there occurs in France a spectacle that captivates the entire nation: the bicycle Tour de France. Glamorous stars . . . a dozen teams, regional or national . . . a month of racing, some twenty stages. A formal start like a military revue or the arrival of a head of state.

Delicious rides followed by great combats, that free rhythm of serious efforts and amused idleness, so characteristic of the French; drama, humor, emotion: such is the prodigious spectacle beginning this summer morning when the great army of racers and onlookers slowly gains momentum.

27

. . . a spectacle that captivates the entire nation . . .

The Frenchman's geography is not that of books, it is that of the Tour; each year, by means of the Tour, he knows the length of his coasts and the height of his mountains. Each year he tallies his frontiers and his products.

By its extension, the Tour is incorporated into the depths of France; in it each Frenchman discovers his own houses and monuments, his provincial present and his ancient past. It has been said the Frenchman is not much of a geographer: his geography is not that of books, it is that of the Tour; each year, by means of the Tour, he knows the length of his coasts and the height of his mountains. Each year he recomposes the material unity of his country, each year he tallies his frontiers and his products.

Such is the theater of combat: all France. It is in the setting of a great war that a whole army of

The racer sets out, alone;

he will ride as fast as

possible every second,

as if there were nothing

in the world but time

and himself.

followers will play the part of the general staff and the commissariat. This army has its generals who stand, eyes fixed on the horizon. It has its light cavalry, entrusted with liaisons, it has its thinkers and its mathematicians . . . it has its gymnasts . . . its historians . . . and its press correspondents.

It also, and especially, has its commissariat, its heavy convoys loaded with supplies, machines, or food. For always, without stopping, men must eat and drink.

As in old wartime images, someone hands the marching combatant something to drink. . . . And even if the racers cannot drink wine, wine

This combat is a competition, it is not a conflict. Which means that man must conquer not man but the resistance of things.

must be present in the Tour, for the Tour is all France. This great monthlong war consists of successive campaigns. Each day has its battle, each night its victor: water, flowers, kisses . . . all this before the day's winner dons the yellow ritual insignia of his victory. War has its peaceful moments, the Tour its happy ones: as in the earliest combats, at evening weapons are suspended, once more everything becomes peaceable: this is the warrior's rest, these are the warrior's ministrations.

There is the dance on the public square . . . the crowd strolling and diverted by the sight of the enormous publicity cortège that follows the Tour.

Each day has its battle, each night its victor:

water, flowers, kisses . . . all this before the day's

winner dons the yellow ritual insignia of his victory.

There is the narrative of the day's epic, which the Tour broadcasts across all France, for the Tour has its writers . . . its inspired poets. Elsewhere there is the combatants' fraternal meal, the winner's commentary, the silence of those who are defeated. Finally there is the preparation of tomorrow's weapons. For tomorrow, at sunrise, everything must begin again.

Because the Tour is not only a splendid story, it is also a serious struggle. A struggle against what? Against men and teams, of course. But as almost always in sports, this combat is a

competition, it is not a conflict. Which means that man must conquer not man but the resistance of things.

And this combat is so much everyone's business that in the Tour, men's mutual assistance overflows the barriers of the spectacle, and of the combat: not only does the crowd actively participate in the racers' effort, it assists them, feeds them, races with them . . .

But the rivals themselves unite when one of them seems likely to give up the race. For that is the stake of the Tour: to hold out. To hold out against anger, against suffering. To hold out,

The rivals themselves unite when one of them seems likely to give up the race. For that is the stake of the Tour: to hold out. To hold out against anger, against suffering. To hold out, which means to begin again.

There are the winners. . . .

There are the unlucky

ones. . . . There is despair.

There is self-control.

which means to begin again. The racer's real enemy is time. Time is usually other men's time. But sometimes, in certain cruel stages, it is pure time, watch time.

The racer sets out, alone; he will ride as fast as possible every second, as if there were nothing in the world but time and himself. He never *feels* his victory. It is his watch that abstractly tells him of it, and it is because, in this sport, resistance proceeds from things and not from men, that men can so easily help each other, even when they fight each other. . . . To help each other—sometimes to slow down and wait for each other—and occa-

War has its peaceful moments. At evening weapons are suspended, once more everything becomes peaceable: this is the warrior's rest, these are the warrior's ministrations.

39

sionally even to give each other a push. For the stake of the combat is not to know who will defeat the other, who will destroy the other, but who will best subjugate that third common enemy: nature. Heat, cold, it is these excesses, and worse still their opposites, which the racer must confront with an even, inflexible movement; it is Earth's resistance he must add to the resistance of objects . . .

The severest ordeal that nature imposes on the racer is the mountain. The mountain: weight. Now to conquer the slopes and the weight of things is to allow that man can possess the entire physical universe. But this conquest is so arduous that a moral man must commit himself to it altogether; that is why—and the whole country knows this—the mountain stages are the key to the Tour: not only because they determine the winner, but because they openly manifest the nature of the stake, the meaning of the combat, the virtues of the combatant.

It is not muscle that wins. What wins is a certain idea

of man and of the world, of man in the world . . .

The end of a mountain stage is therefore a condensation of the entire human adventure:

There are the winners. . . . There are the unlucky ones. . . . There is despair. There is self-control.

Muscle does not make the sport: that is the evidence of the Tour de France. Muscle, however precious, is never anything more than raw material. It is not muscle that wins. What wins is a certain idea of man and of the world, of man in the world. This idea is that man is fully defined by his action, and man's action is not to dominate other men, it is to dominate things.

43

Of all sports-loving countries, Canada is one of the most often frozen, yet of all "pedestrian" sports ice hockey is the fastest: sport is this specific power to transform each thing into its opposite. And it is in this renewed miracle that a whole country participates, by its crowds, its press, radio, television: behind the scenes, before the combat, however fierce, there is the physical relation of a country and its inhabitants.

What is a national sport? It is a sport that rises out of the substance of a nation, out of its

The children seem to be fighting, but they are

merely learning to inhabit their country.

soil and climate. To play hockey is constantly to repeat that men have transformed motionless winter, the hard earth, and suspended life, and that precisely out of all this they have made a swift, vigorous, passionate sport.

The children seem to be fighting, but they are merely learning to inhabit their country, and what the mothers' eyes follow in their progeny's first adult gestures is not so much the outcome of a battle as the development of an initiation. This first law of the climate is entirely contained by the gesture that prepares the space of the combat: a little frozen water, and hockey is possible.

This first law of the climate is entirely contained by the gesture that prepares the space of the combat: a little frozen water, and hockey is possible.

Sport is the entire

trajectory separating

a combat from a riot.

All that remains is to make this space into the object of a rule: of a strategy, of an idea. In this rapid sport, thought can be only a reflex, and this reflex learned like any other. All foreseeable maneuvers become the object of a lesson: to seize the puck in flight and then to conduct it through a thousand obstacles; in this fashion one learns to score a goal . . . and even to stop.

Here is everything that will occur in the game that now begins. One rule dominates the game: that no player penetrate the opposing side ahead of the puck; whence the irresistible, liberating aspect of these great collective deployments. It is as if the men were sucked up less by the opposing goal than by the malicious object that leads them to it. The spectators' choral manifestations punctuate the duration of the match. By its massive exclamations the crowd comments on the spectacle. Every moral value can be invested in the sport: endurance, self-possession, temerity, courage. The great players are heroes, not stars.

A goal scored is, as in all sports, a great victory, but in hockey the game is so fast, the puck so tiny, that a failed goal is not only a defeat, it is virtually a wound, intense as a pistol shot: for man's failure is yet more intense in the face of the triumph of ineffable things than in the face of heavy things.

The goal is empty. Why?

Because hockey is a game of offensives, in which the pleasure of attack justifies every risk. Occasionally one team's leader decides to pull the goalie in order to be entitled to increase his attack group by one combatant and thereby to bring the war without intermission into enemy lines.

Man's failure is yet more intense in the face of the triumph of ineffable things than in the face of heavy things.

51

One rule dominates the game: that no player

penetrate the opposing side ahead of the puck;

whence the irresistible, liberating aspect of these

great collective deployments.

By its very power, this sport sustains a permanent threat of illegality: the game constantly risks being faster than consciousness and overwhelming it. There then occurs a kind of test of sport by the absurd: the *sport scandal.* This scandal occurs when men collapse the slender barrier separating the two combats: that of sport, that of life. Having lost all intermediary space, deprived of stake and rule alike, the players' combat ceases to be subject to the distance without which there can be no human society: once again a game becomes a conflict.

All that remains is to

make this space into

the object of a rule:

of a strategy, of an

idea.

By its very power, this sport sustains a permanent threat of illegality: the game constantly risks being faster than consciousness and overwhelming it.

Then sport returns to the immediate world of passions and aggressions, dragging with it the crowd, which came precisely to seek purification from it. Sport is the entire trajectory separating a combat from a riot.

It's raining in England, yet all England is outdoors. Why? There is a soccer match at Wembley. As in all great sport spectacles, the inaugurating ritual is observed with great formality. At certain periods, in certain societies, the theater has had a major social function: it collected the entire city within a shared experience: the knowledge of its own passions. Today it is sport that in its way performs this function. Except that the city has enlarged: it is no longer a town, it is a country, often

57

What is sport? Sport answers this question

by another question: who is best?

even, so to speak, the whole world; sport is a great
modern institution cast in the ancestral forms of
spectacle.

Why? Why love sport? First, it must be re-
membered that everything happening to the player
also happens to the spectator. But whereas in the
theater the spectator is only a voyeur, in sport he is
a participant, an actor. And then, in sport, man does
not confront man directly. There enters between
them an intermediary, a stake, a machine, a puck,
or a ball. And this thing is the very symbol of
things: it is in order to possess it, to master it, that
one is strong, adroit, courageous. To watch, here,

What need have these men to attack? Why are men disturbed by this spectacle? Why do they commit themselves to it so completely? Why this useless combat? What is sport?

is not only to live, to suffer, to hope, to understand but also, and especially, to say so—by voice, by gesture, by facial expression; it is to call the whole world to witness: in a word, it is to communicate. Ultimately man knows certain forces, certain conflicts, joys and agonies: sport expresses them, liberates them, consumes them without ever letting anything be destroyed.

In sport, man experiences life's fatal combat, but this combat is distanced by the spectacle, reduced to its forms, cleared of its effects, of its dangers, and of its shames: it loses its noxiousness, not its brilliance or its meaning.

What is sport? Sport answers this question by another question: who is best? But to this question of the ancient duels, sport gives a new meaning: for man's excellence is sought here only in relation to things. Who is the best man to overcome the resistance of things, the immobility of nature? Who is the best to work the world, to give it to men . . . to all men? That is what sport says. Occasionally one would like to make sport say something else. But sport is not made for that.

What need have these men to attack? Why are men disturbed by this spectacle? Why do they commit themselves to it so completely? Why this

useless combat? What is sport? What is it then that men put into sport? Themselves, their human universe. Sport is made in order to speak the human contract.

Ultimately man knows certain forces, certain conflicts, joys and agonies: sport expresses them, liberates them, consumes them without ever letting anything be destroyed.

To watch, here, is not only to live, to suffer, to hope, to understand but also, and especially, to say so—by voice, by gesture, by facial expression; it is to call the whole world to witness: in a word, it is to communicate.

65

CORRESPONDENCE

Letter from Hubert Aquin to Roland Barthes

Montréal, April 4, 1960

Dear Monsieur Barthes

I am soon to begin creating an hourlong film on the subject of sport. My intention is to produce not a history of sport but rather, let us say, its phenomenology and its poetics.

You have already guessed that your first chapter of *Mythologies* was of great interest to me, and that this letter is a request for you to write the commentary of my film. But there is more than one coincidence involved, for I have read a number of your texts and agree with your vision of reality; by such "reality" I mean "In the Ring" and "Racine" as well as "The Tour de France" . . .

The film I am to create will appear in a documentary series of the National Film Bureau entitled "Comparisons."

A preestablished formula therefore obliges me to construct the film around three or four major sports practiced in different countries. With this in mind, I have already made a first choice of several national sports: car races in Italy, the Tour de France bicycle race, soccer in Hungary or bullfights in Spain, hockey in Canada. This selection is not definitive from the sports-analysis viewpoint, and you will tell me yourself if it is meaningful. For the film's goal is to understand sport, to apprehend from a new rational aspect this social and poetic phenomenon which produces on the public a veritable amorous crystallization.

Not one image of this film has been shot, or even collected (for I envision the utilization of stock shots). I am still at the stage of conception. For precisely this reason, if you agree to write a commentary on the finished product, I should like you to participate in its birth, its initial orientation. And here is how: write me, as soon as you can, what you think of the subject in general and of its orientation, and tell me as well how you yourself imagine the construction of the film.

After such a preliminary report, I would ask you to specify the screenplay according to certain data. As far as research into existing footage to consider is concerned and with regard to certain strictly documentary matters, I shall excuse you if you haven't the time to give to such matters. This tedious part of the work can be accomplished without you.

For the final commentary you will write (in about six or eight months) once the film is put together, you would receive a payment of $1,000. For the initial reports establishing the outlines of the screenplay and orienting the film's realization, the payment would be about $250.

I don't believe that the Ocean between us should be an obstacle to an effective collaboration. At the start, everything will be done by correspondence, but at a certain point in our work, I look forward to meeting you.

I hope that the project of such a film will interest you, and as I need to know if it does, you will be kind to let me know of your decision as soon as you have made it.

Please accept, dear Monsieur Barthes, the expression of my warmest feelings.

Hubert Aquin

Director-producer.

Letter from Hubert Aquin to Roland Barthes

Montréal, August 3, 1960

Dear Monsieur Barthes

Here are some remarks that will bring you up to date on my work's progress. Some of them require an answer from you.

1) In the course of various readings, I have experienced an imperative need to justify the choice of our five sports. There is no question of an exhaustive enu-

meration, nor of a history, but let us say of a selection. But here too, a specification is necessary: we are dealing only with spectator sports, and we are setting aside athletic or Olympic or even solitary sport. What concerns us (I must agree that I am deducing this from a quasi-intuitive initial choice) is sport as a psychosocial phenomenon; it is not sport in isolation but sport in its professional aspect almost exclusively; for all spectator sports are, in a more or less organized fashion, professional.

2) The plan of the film. I have wondered whether we should envisage a treatment by sports or by chapters. The disadvantage of dividing the documentary into four sports is to keep coming back, apropos of each one, to certain descriptive notions. Hence there is a certain danger of repetition or rather of dullness. On the other hand, the other solution—to proceed analytically by functions—involves a risk of didacticism. Furthermore, I fear that this dialectical approach will deprive the public of an emotive impact that can be delivered more certainly after a ten- or twelve-minute dive into the universe of a single sport. Unless there is an inter-

mediate solution (which I have not found) which seems more flexible, I would opt for a sport-by-sport division.

3) In order not to discuss, apropos of each sport, all the various functions you enumerated in your first outline, it would be good to speak exhaustively thoroughly of each function just once. In practical terms, we must establish a scale of predominance of functions in relation to each sport. For example: the cosmic function is richer in the Tour than in hockey, where almost all the competitions, even between high school teams, take place in indoor stadiums.

What I need, right now, are very simple indications that would permit me, in each sport, to emphasize one or some more meaningful aspects without thereby surrendering a general outline of the functions it expresses. The "fantasmatic" function, to take another example, seems to me closely linked to bullfighting and to car racing, in which accidents, most often, are synonymous with death. Are not soccer and hockey obvious "moral epitomes"? In other words, tell me whether I should continue in this direction.

4) In your first note, you suggested making a brief historical sketch of sport. I have not yet looked for visual documents to illustrate such a chapter; but I suppose I would have to use old prints. On the subject of this historical résumé, I have asked myself the following question: does not sport as art, so to speak, undergo transformations with time, does it not age along with the period or the civilization in which it is born? In this regard, the Olympic Games are the equivalent, in our own day, of the Greco-Roman academicism in sculpture, for instance. Bullfighting itself, so plainly archaic, continues atrophying (the size of the bulls has considerably diminished, the violence of the spectacle has been attenuated and even dismissed). The golden age of bicycle racing seems already over. Car races, on the other hand, have never been so popular. Fencing was a great sport two centuries ago. Is there not a relation to be established, a correspondence between the apogee of a sport and its sociohistorical implantation?

5) You say that there is no eroticism in sport. Quite right. Yet in Greece women were banned from the stadium; in the Middle Ages and until recently

they were singularly absent from sport. The universe of sport is almost exclusively male.

6) Coenesthesia. Here is one of the interesting notions to be developed in our film. I hope to find adequate footing to illustrate it, but could you tell me, approximately, whether you intend to speak at any length about this notion. Do you consider coenesthesia as the spectator's privileged mode of identification with the player? If so, this function, well illustrated, becomes the obvious occasion to speak to the public. There is also the "ancient chorus" aspect of the public: shouts, clapping, sighs, which essentially express the public's participation in a theatrical as in a sport spectacle. Is there such a thing?

7) I have reread what you wrote about the Tour de France in *Mythologies,* and I have every intention of taking all the inspiration I can from this classic description.

As I remarked in an earlier letter, I will keep up a massive scrutiny of sport footage. Would you be kind enough, meanwhile, to send me brief answers to the several questions I have raised in this letter?

Till our next, dear Monsieur Barthes, and please accept the expression of my warmest feelings.

HUBERT AQUIN

Hubert Aquin's letters to Roland Barthes have been published in Aquin's *Journal, 1948–1971* (Montréal, Bibliothèque québécois, 1999). Our thanks to Andrée Yanacopoulo for permission to reprint these letters here.

TRANSLATOR'S AFTERWORD

A Backward Echo

I had become a friend of Roland Barthes some four years before he wrote this text, which was not included in either version of Le Seuil's edition of the French author's *Oeuvres complètes* (three 1,500-page volumes in 1995, five 1,000-page volumes in 2002); I had heard his voice (on the telephone) in 1957 before I even knew Roland Barthes's name, and the resonance of it has remained quite distinct in my ears, though there will be no more of those peculiarly *vocal* transatlantic phone calls in which the baffled translator would pester the similarly baffled author for a reference, a source—"You cite—in French—a sentence from Hobbes, Roland—where can I find the original?" "No idea, *mon petit Richard;* just make the English sound like Hobbes"—and so vivid is the resonance that once again I suffer one of those shocks of the impossible recognition that Roland died twenty-seven years ago; after all, in the course of those nearly three decades

I've translated several of his most remarkable books *after* Roland himself had been run down by a laundry truck on the Rue des Écoles in 1980, and one might suppose the authorial audition would become familiar: familiar but hardly accustomed. . . . Hearing his voice yet again (as the translator—especially the persisting translator of many of Roland's books over many years—must hear His Master's Voice during all those hours of trying to register what he hears) while I translated this brilliant little text written for a Canadian "documentary" in 1960–1961, I cannot resist a couple of observations on what you have read.

In 1957, just before I met him, Barthes had written two essays on sport in his popular *Mythologies* sequence, one on wrestling and one, proleptically as it turned out, on "the Tour de France as Epic": "The Tour possesses a veritable Homeric geography. As in the Odyssey, the race here is both a periplus of ordeals and a total exploration of the earth's limits. Ulysses reached the ends of the earth several times. The Tour, too, frequently grazes an inhuman world . . . and if we were to refer to some Viconian schema of history, the Tour would represent in it that ambiguous moment when man strongly personifies Nature in order to confront it more readily and to liberate himself more completely."

One sees "readily" enough that Barthes, having completed (after many requested extensions) his "mythologies"—that Marxist social register of petit-bourgeois frauds and frivolities—would gladly move on to another tonality altogether, one that characteristically "runs" to a very long sentence, a rumination held together by colons and various signs of equivalence ("in other words," "that is," "in short"); clearly he is reluctant, after all that semijournalistic roughing-up, to let his sentence go until, like Jacob's angel, it turns and blesses him. That blessing is idiosyncratic to the max—one hears the man's voice throughout, intimate but not personal, responsible but not officious, convincing but not accusatory, and at first glance these long chains of colons may seem merely willful. But this is not the case, for despite its circumstantial genesis (as in *Le Sport et les hommes,* only four years on) Barthes's ulterior work is what historians used to call a progress, an integral occasion of growth, the account of a mind changing; hence its apprehension of *membership* (it is the colon's literal task: a *colonizing* of pertinence) is crucial to its goal.

To invert Buffon: *cet homme, c'est le style.*

Consider the last words of this commentary on national sports, finishing up with hockey in Canada: *What need have these men to attack? Why are men disturbed by this spectacle? Why do they commit themselves to it so completely? Why this useless combat? What is sport? What is it then that men put into sport? Themselves, their human universe. Sport is made in order to speak the human contract.* I wonder how the sports lovers of Montréal responded to the Montaigne-like rhythms of this *essai,* when it was recited above the dire events on the screen. And even how American *readers* will take (though they have been much forewarned by Roland's admirers and imitators in the meanwhile) to this bare-faced plurality of signification, the indulged suspension of meaning? How often we need to be assured of what we know in the old ways of knowing—how seldom we can afford to venture beyond the pale into that chromatic fantasy where, as Rilke said (in 1908), "begins the revision of categories, where something past comes again, as though out of the future; something formerly accomplished as something to be completed." (A just description, by the way, of the work in hand.) In this very essay (perhaps this is why it has not found its way into the Complete Works), we see Barthes's spoken words becoming *writerly,* and now that we know what lies ahead in his generous production, we may be less dismayed, even here, by the terms he has come to (he usually assumes Greek has a word for it) in which his discoveries must be rendered. For Barthes's text is *writerly,* his divagations (I use Mallarmé's term advisedly, for it is with Mallarmé, Barthes has said, that our "modernity" begins) are a new achievement of the literature of criticism. It makes upon us strenuous demands, such criticism, it makes exactions. And because of them, precisely, we too are released, reprieved; we are free to read *knowing the reason why.* Essentially an erotic meditation, because it concerns what is inexpressible (is that not the essence of eros?), Barthes's little essay is a modest and intimate and suggestive and *useful* account of what, in my imbecilic *readerly* fashion, I had always supposed to be a frivolous activity.

I suppose, now, that this is where I must introduce what would have been— no, what *was* the final efflorescence of Roland Barthes's fertile career, for I feel it to have been suggested and even prepared for on every page of this little enchiridion of human striving and strife.

In 1974, fifteen years before the first theatrical screening of *Le Sport et les hommes,* Barthes presented his French editor with a sort of autobiography, a little book that describes that part of his life—his tastes, his childhood, his body then and now, his education, his passions and regrets—which a man knows to have gone into his work. And thereby it is a part of his work, and a clarification; it is in fact the working-out, as the psychoanalyst would say, of the man's life in his works, and of the man's works in his life. And when Barthes delivered the book to his editor he specified—and the specification applied to all the translations of *Roland Barthes par Roland Barthes*—that on the flyleaf, in a reproduction of his own handwriting, must appear this sentence: *Tout ceci doit être considéré comme dit par un personnage de roman:* It must all be considered as if spoken by a character in a novel.

This was the first premonition of what was to become—in a lecture given in 1980 at the Humanities Institute of New York University, introduced by Susan

Sontag (and I need not remind you of that critic's latterly and definitive "turn to fiction")—Roland Barthes's scandalous indication, in a discussion ostensibly of "Proust and Names," that he was contemplating—did he mean writing? dreaming? kidding?—a novel!

But he had already written it, or them—in *Roland Barthes by Roland Barthes,* in *Camera Lucida* (so described by no less a reader than Jacques Derrida), and finally in *Incidents,* that last desperate effort to assign his life sufficient value to the man living it, an adequation only to be obtained by *being read.* All this, I contend, can be discerned, by the wonders of that developing fluid we call *the years,* in the little text in your hands to which I also commend your attention for its own sake.

RICHARD HOWARD

PHOTO CREDITS